Birds Arou
Surrey

Derek Belsey

I dedicate this book to the next
generation – my grandchildren
Rosie, Molly, Luke and Isabella.

Contents

Above: A little picture of Little Grebes

Front Cover: Tawny Owls.

Title Page: A Redshank cautiously approaches its nest.

Introduction: The Reed Warbler feeds a young Cuckoo.

Back Cover: A Young Dunnock.

All photographs are by the author with the exception of some by Cliff Reddick.

ISBN 0 9530734 32
© Derek Belsey 2002

Published by Derek Belsey
Tel: 01932 241886

Designed by
Robert Antell-Abbey Graphics.
Printed by Ian Allan Printing Ltd.

Introduction

I have kept this introduction short, enabling me to squeeze in as many stories and new photographs as possible.

The reason for this, my third book is, since I started writing a monthly article in the *Surrey Herald* newspaper some two years ago and more recently, the *Village Echo,* I've received many calls and letters. Most have been questions and sightings on birds, but many people have also asked "When was I going to write another book".

This has been very flattering, but as I've mentioned in my previous books, putting pen to paper does not come naturally to me, but after much deliberation I decided that maybe we do need a more educational book on our local birdlife. This I have tried to achieve with some factual stories, the odd poem and as many new photographs as space allows.

I obviously cannot cover every species around Surrey, but by giving an overall picture, for a two and a half year period from January 2000 hopefully my book will show what birds still exist in these areas. Also by writing the text in a diary vein, I'm able to mention some of the people who have contacted me over this period of time and this is my way of thanking them for their contributions towards this book.

Five of The Best

JANUARY

JANUARY is a good month to watch five members of the Thrush family.

The sixth, the Ring Ouzel, arrives here later in the spring, although you would be very lucky to see one in this area.

But you can see our two other visitors from Northern Europe, the Fieldfare and the smaller Redwing, which are in the area at this moment.

When they arrive, usually you can be pretty sure that we will be in for a cold snap.

Both species love berries and if the weather becomes severe they are not averse to searching gardens for food.

So if you have any berry-bearing bushes in yours, keep an eye out for them. Also, cut up some old apples and throw them about the garden for they are also partial to the odd Granny Smith!

Other favourite places to watch for them are in local parks and surrounding fields.

I saw a flock of some 80 Redwings and a few Fieldfares in the fields adjacent to Cowey Sale last weekend.

The third member of the family is the Blackbird, which at this time of the year is busily singing to attract a mate, in between the odd sparring session with rival cock Blackbirds.

The fourth member, the Song Thrush, is very much on the decline for various reasons.

The Magpie accounts for the loss of eggs and young from the thrushes' nests.

Slug pellets kill off their main food supply – snails!

Our gardens may look pretty without slugs and snails but they are very quiet without the Song Thrush.

Last but not least, is my favourite, the Mistle Thrush, which is, in my opinion, the best songster of them all.

Left: A cock Blackbird feeds his hungry offspring.

Above right: Mistle Trush at the nest.

Lower right: The Song Thrush sings above

Larger than the Song Thrush, he will sing from dawn to dusk from the top of the tallest tree.

The windier the weather, the better he will sing, hence his nickname, the Stormcock.

The Magpies also take a share of their eggs and young but many survive because the Mistle Thrush will defend its nest at any cost.

It gives me great satisfaction to watch a victorious Mistle Thrush seeing off a pair of merciless Magpies.

They are also one of our earlier nesting birds and in a good year, will raise two broods.

So when you're out and about, look out for the berry-bearing bushes, keep an eye on the tallest trees and go easy on the slug pellets this spring.

5

A redwing rests in the Winter sunshine.

Grateful Grebes and Gravel Pits

FEBRUARY

IT'S nice to be able to write about a bird that is on the increase, not just locally but in most parts of Britain.

Just over 100 years ago Great Crested Grebes suffered huge losses as their feathers were a prime target for decorating ladies' hats.

So much so that there were fewer than 40 pairs left in the whole of England.

They are now protected birds and in a breeding season, there are now more than 4,000 pairs.

Although a lot of people are anti-gravel raising, the increase in the Grebe population is partly due to the extra habitat that pits provide.

As I live by the side of one, this time of year I often lay in bed at night listening to the Grebes calling, before starting in the following weeks, some of the most fascinating courtship displays and dances.

At the start of their mating ritual, both birds gather weed from the bed of the gravel pit and still holding it in their beaks, shake their heads from side-to-side before swimming away from one another.

Sometimes they "run" together over the water, then suddenly dive below the surface. This is commonly known as the weed dance.

Often a mating platform is made for copulation, after which both birds build it up with more weed to form a floating nest that is usually anchored to a submerged branch or reeds.

After the eggs are laid, both birds share the incubation for up to 28 days. Once the chicks are all hatched they climb aboard their parents' backs for warmth and safety.

If you are out walking beside one of our gravel pits or even the River Thames and you spot a pair of Grebes, take a close look and you may catch a glimpse of the chicks as they poke their heads from beneath the feathers of mum and dad, looking for their next fish supper.

Right: An ever alert Grebe.

The Grebe settles down on its eggs.

Once you have seen this I'm sure you will return for a repeat performance.

One site that I return to each year is beside Chertsey Bridge, next to The Bridge Lodge.

On February 15th 1998 I was lucky enough to photograph the first Grebe chick born in the whole of Britain that year.

I made my first visit this year on Sunday morning, 30th January, to see the manager of The Bridge Lodge, David Burns, who had phoned me the previous day about my feature in the *Surrey Herald* newspaper, only to find one of the Grebes already sitting on eggs.

I phoned the British Trust for Ornithology and it seems that our Grebes have done it again, probably the first to nest in Britain this year.

If you pay a "careful" visit to see our star birds you may even catch me having a "swift half" while pursuing my hobby and who knows, you may be lucky enough to see the first Grebe chick born in this year.

Meanwhile remember, no longer do Grebe feathers adorn ladies' hats at Royal Ascot, but many Great Crested Grebes gratefully adorn our local gravel pits and rivers.

Their chick receives a meal.

My pair of early nesting Grebes.

Their Feathered Nest is The Best

MARCH

MY bird for March is the Long-Tailed Tit, or as it is sometimes called by older country folk, the Bottle Tit.

The reason could be the shape of the nest, which is oval, with an entrance hold at the top.

When built, it's a work of art with both birds working together on a construction made up of lichen, animal hair and cobwebs.

Somehow they manage to line it with up to 2,000 feathers.

This I've always found amazing but, more so, the fact that eight to 12 eggs are laid.

Often when I find a nest and one of the birds is incubating (usually the female), it sometimes pops its head out to look around and because the nest is built just big enough for both bird and eggs, its tail is bent up and over its head.

This looks quite funny as it appears that the bird is wearing a flat cap.

When the chicks hatch it is not uncommon for other Long-Tailed Tits to help out in the feeding, usually because they have had an unsuccessful nesting attempt of their own.

Which reminds me of something similar that happened in my garden a few years ago.

I had a pair of Blue Tits nesting in one of my bird boxes but one of them was taken by a Sparrowhawk, leaving its mate to feed the young Blue Tits on its own.

But to my astonishment, a pair of Long-Tailed Tits started to help out. Unfortunately, this caused the Blue Tit to eventually desert its family.

The Long-Tailed Tits carried out their fostering duties until the Sparrowhawk struck again.

The remaining Long-Tailed Tit could not cope on its own and the young blue tits left the nest with not much chance of survival.

I carefully watched the outcome, which was not very encouraging as the Jays took most of them. I saved just three young, which I attempted to hand rear, but to no avail.

Nature can be very cruel at times but one little bird's death means another bird's survival.

Getting back to a successful pair of Long-Tailed Tits, when the young leave the nest they stay close together as a family throughout the summer.

Come late autumn, whole flocks of them will join up with other Tits and Finches on feeding sessions as they fly from tree to tree.

During the winter months they often huddle together on a branch in groups to keep warm at night.

Those that survive will pair up and at this time of year, will again be on the search for 2,000 feathers!

P.S. Lots of Goldcrests and Siskins about this month. The Great Crested Grebe at Chertsey Bridge has done it again with one very early newly-hatched chick. Lisa and Christian of the Bridge Lodge are keeping me informed of its progress.

Left: A tight squeeze.

A colourful picture.

Wonderful Wheatears, Stunning Stonechats

APRIL

THE month of April has once again been disastrous for our birds. The wet and cold weather has dampened a lot of their mating instincts, with quite a few abandoning nests and eggs.

The pair of swans that nest each year near Chertsey Bridge have lost their eggs due to flooding. Most of the blue tits and great tits have slowed down on nest building in my nest boxes but hopefully, with a few days of dry and warmer weather, they will start again in earnest.

Looking on the brighter side, it was nice to see, although wet and bedraggled, a few Wheatears and a pair of Stonechats.

The Wheatears were obviously stopping off for a feed before continuing their journey to nesting grounds further north.

The Stonechats were a real bonus as they are a bird that has virtually disappeared from our area. The last pair I found nesting locally was some 10 years ago in a small area of gorse at Halliford. The nearest place I know to watch them now is Horsell Common or, further afield, Chobham Common.

The cock bird cannot be mistaken when perched up showing his black head and back, white patches on neck, wings and rump, with a brilliant chestnut breast. He is a handsome bird as he sings to attract a mate but if disturbed will let out a warning call "tsak-tsak," before disappearing into surrounding undergrowth.

The Wheatears, as I mentioned, are en route to nesting grounds, but if you are lucky enough to see one you will never forget it as it is a beautifully-marked bird.

Stunning Stonechat.

Above: Wonderful Wheatear.

Right: Traffic light Mistle Thrush.

   The male is magnificent with a white rump, a
bluish grey back, black wings and facial mask
with buff-coloured breast feathers.
   I have been fortunate enough to watch their
mating behaviour while visiting the Shetland
Islands one spring. Both birds face one another,
with the male puffing up his feathers to jump up
and down in the air before throwing himself down
on the ground with his head, wing and tail feathers
stretched out. A sight I shall always remember.
   I have read that years ago thousands were
trapped as they roosted on the the south coast,
only to be served up on Victorian dinner tables.
   Fortunately times have changed, so keep a look
out for the wonderful Wheatear and hopefully the
stunning Stonechat – weather permitting!

P.S. A pair of Mistle-Thrushes reared three young
      in a traffic light (on the amber) in Staines.
      One way of beating the wet weather I
      suppose!

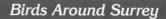

Love Among The Brambles

MAY

ALONG with the smaller Willow Warbler, the Whitethroat is one of our most common visiting Warblers and my favourite site to watch them is on scrubland by Shepperton by-pass.

Each year, they return from South Africa with the males arriving first to compete for this small remaining piece of habitat.

They are beautiful little birds, the male being more prominent with his grey cap and seemingly whiter throat.

Because they are not as secretive as most other Warblers, from behind some cover I can observe the whole of their courtship behaviour.

The cock bird will perch up on a high bush or bramble, singing his short but melodious song to attract a mate.

The first pair I saw together seemed to be waging a territorial fight, but after watching for a while I realised it was a courtship display.

Still singing, the male would dart towards her with nesting material in his beak as though it was an attack. She then spread her wings and tail feathers out to see him off.

This procedure went on for some time before she finally accepted one of the trial nests he had partly built since his arrival. I returned the next day to watch both birds completing the structure of the nest deep down in some long grass. This year, I watched it all again with the added bonus of seeing several skirmishes with some neighbouring Reed Buntings.

She laid five eggs, and while she incubated them I moved my hide gradually towards the nest.

After the young Whitethroats hatched, she would slip off to collect food along with her mate, always returning secretly through the undergrowth to the back of the nest.

The male perched on a nearby stalk every time before dropping in to feed their ever hungry family. All five were fledged successfully and after I removed the hide I sat back to watch them being fed away from the nest.

The male bird came to scold me a few times, so I left them in peace.

In late September or early October, the Whitethroats flew over Shepperton by-pass on their way back to South Africa.

As usual I will eagerly be awaiting their return next spring.

Left: A very cautious male.

Right: The female Whitethroat looks over her young family.

Delightful Dabchicks

JUNE

THE Dabchick, or Little Grebe as it's commonly known, is a secretive bird and normally the only sign of its presence is the sound of a "plop" in the water.

Malcolm, a friend of mine, is a keen trout fisherman and on more than a few occasions, has cast his fly to one of these plops, thinking it was a fish rising, only to see a Dabchick show itself briefly before disappearing from sight.

I've spent many hours watching their amusing courtship displays, which at times can become very vocal.

Both male and female face one another on the water before going into a trilling song and diving below the surface.

After several days of these performances they build a floating nest, very similar to their bigger cousin, the Great Crested Grebe, but usually more hidden.

Four to six eggs are laid, with both birds sharing the incubating period for about 24 days.

When the chicks hatch they can swim almost immediately, but they mostly use the warmth and security of their parents' backs.

Because Dabchicks are small birds (nine inches) they feed on very small fish, dragonfly nymphs, shrimps and various water insects.

The pair of birds that I've managed to watch and photograph for the past three years have been partial to tadpoles and small newts.

This has been very rewarding for two reasons. Firstly, it's not easy to find these little pockets of water with their own population of newts anymore. Secondly, the Dabchicks are neighbours to a special pair of Tufted Ducks that I've written about on page 68. So if you want to see a delightful Little Grebe, look out for a quiet pocket of water and listen for the sound of a distinctive plop.

P.S. Most of the spring visitors have now arrived in our area, such as Sedge Warblers, Reed Warblers, Willow Warblers, Blackcaps, Whitethroats, Chiffchaffs, Reed Buntings, Yellow Wagtails, Little Ringed Plovers, Ringed Plovers etc. And there has been a first for me locally, a wading bird called a Bar-Tailed Godwit.

Left: Three of the chicks wait for their parents to return.

Right: A proud parent and its first chick.

Sedge Warblers Showtime

JUNE

AS I write this month's bird article the temperature is in the mid-eighties and it's hard to believe that May was one of the wettest on record.

Most birds had a rough time, with Blue Tits and Great Tits heading the casualty list.

Because of the continuous rain, their food chain was dramatically affected. The Blue Tits in my bird boxes were taking bread from the bird table to feed their young because of the shortage of insects and caterpillars.

Many birds lost their broods and those that managed to survive had to face the weather, not to mention the Magpies and Jays.

One of my bird boxes was attacked by a pair of Great Spotted Woodpeckers and it was only a rather speedily made-up cage of chicken wire around the box that deterred the Woodpeckers from taking the young blue tits.

Now the weather has improved and so have the chances of our visiting warblers. A pair of Sedge Warblers that I've been watching makes a happier story.

They arrive each year from Africa to claim a territory for breeding.

Although they are called Sedge Warblers, they seem to have no preference for sedge and will nest in most vegetation or undergrowth, usually near water.

Left: Both birds look in.

Above: A curious parent.

Because of this, they are very vulnerable to Cuckoos, who find their nests more easily than some other birds.

My pair nested in some nettles, which I find is one of their favourite nesting sites.

When they arrive the males, like other Warblers, take up vantage points to "sing and dance," to attract a mate. I say sing and dance because the male flies up and down while still singing.

This is something special to watch if there are several cock birds in the area. It is also very confusing as they disappear quickly into the undergrowth before showing themselves again.

When a female has finally accepted his "flying cabarets," up to six eggs are laid, of which she does most of the incubating.

Both birds collect all sorts of insects to feed their young before they leave the nest after about 14 days. That's the time I stop watching them as you need more than one pair of eyes to keep track of their whereabouts, but next year I will again await their return and a repeat performance of a "Sedge Warbler's cabaret."

The Hunter at My Table

JULY

THIS month has been particularly eventful, starting with Sally, the landlady of the Old Manor House Inn, telling me about a pair of Great Crested Grebes that were nesting just a few feet out from the bank of the Thames at Walton.

They became the main topic of conversation among people who walked past the nest, and I received plenty of phone calls on the Grebes' progress.

The female seemed quite at ease with anyone who stopped to look at her – even those with cameras. One such person was Nigel Choat, a professional photographer who came all the way from Guildford to capture this unique bird on film. I obviously did not miss this opportunity to put my camera into action.

As I mentioned in a previous article, the Great Crested Grebe was once persecuted for its feathers but is now a protected bird. Which leads me on to this month's chosen bird, the Sparrowhawk, which was also persecuted by gamekeepers until it was given legal protection in 1966.

When I moved to this area 30 years ago, it was quite rare to see a Sparrowhawk, but now most garden bird tables come under attack by these birds throughout the year. I think it's their way of counter-balancing the loss of hunting habitat and the decline of smaller wild birds.

This year, I've found no fewer than seven nesting pairs locally. My favourite pair nested in an old apple tree by the side of the Abbey River at Chertsey, only yards away from a pair of Kingfishers. Like most Sparrowhawks, four eggs were laid which were incubated for around 35 days.

When the young hatched and were about five days old, I started to notice the adult birds were different from other Sparrowhawks I've watched. The mother

Left: Mealtime over!

20

seldom brooded the chicks but seemed content to keep a watch over them from a nearby branch.

Above: Not much room in the nest!

Below: The Great Crested Grebe was a talking point.

The cock bird still brought prey to the empty nest when the young had left and were being enticed by the female to hunt for themselves. Occasionally, one would come back to the silent larder for a quick snack.

Another family I've been watching nested at St George's Hill golf course, where I sometimes play. Usually, Sparrowhawks hunt small birds but will kill anything up to the size of a Pigeon.

I witnessed one such kill the other Sunday morning. Peter, a playing partner of mine, pointed out a bird fluttering on the side of the fairway. I ran over for a closer look to find a fully-fledged Hawk standing on possibly its first solo kill.

Its prey was a young Wood Pigeon that was probably on its first solo flight. The Hawk did not want to lose its dinner as, on my approach, it tried to pull the Pigeon along the ground.

I was too late to save the Pigeon, so I carried on with the golf. Later, I returned to the scene of the kill, where just a pile of feathers were blowing in the wind.

Jewel of Our Waterways

AUGUST

WHEN I'm giving illustrated talks, the question most often asked is: "How and where can I see a Kingfisher?"

Well, a pair of Kingfishers do nest somewhere along the River Ash, but unless you know the location, the chances of seeing one will be remote, but if you sit quietly on almost any of our local gravel pits you will improve your chances considerably.

If a pair are nesting and feeding their young they will be flying about the water all day long looking for small fish. Also, look out for a steep bank as that is where they like to dig out their nesting tunnel.

If you find one, watch from a distance so as not to disturb or alarm the birds.

I think that the Kingfisher is our most colourful bird, brilliant turquoise blue with almost golden brown breast feathers.

There has been a pair nesting close to Laleham farm for the past ten years, but they thought better of it this year as a pair of Sparrowhawks nested above their bank.

The Kingfishers on the gravel pit at the back of my house lost their nesting site as the bank collapsed into the water last winter. But that turned out to be a bonus, as they have returned to their original nesting site just 30 yards from my back garden.

Earlier this year I was talking to one of the anglers who fish the gravel pit as two Kingfishers landed on his fishing rods, both at the same time, now that's being in the right place at the right time!

We have in my area at least six nesting pairs

Left: A little gem.

Above: Turquoise rear view.

Right: Jewel in the sunset.

which, in a good year, raise two broods.

No matter how dull a day may seem, just a glimpse of that turquoise blue will always brighten it up.

Long may the jewel of our waterways shine.

Now You See It, Now You Don't !

SEPTEMBER

ONE of the strangest birds I've watched over the past years is the Nightjar. They arrive from Africa in mid-May to breed in heathland at such places as Horsell and Chobham Common.

Unless you know where they nest it's almost impossible to see one in the daytime as they lay on the ground, resembling a piece of old wood or dead leaves.

The nest is an unlined scrape in the ground, which usually has bits of wood around it to camouflage the sitting bird.

The female lays two eggs that have grey marbled markings. They are incubated mostly by her for about 18 days. When the young are hatched they are fed at night by both parents and leave the nest after a week, staying in the vicinity until they are ready to fly.

Some birds have two broods in a good year. Most Nightjars return to the same area each

Below: Head on!

year so when you have located a pair, watching them becomes quite easy.

Dusk is the best time to watch as this is when they leave their daytime roost. The cockbird starts his song (I use the term lightly) which is a churring sound similar to the noise a fishing reel makes when the ratchet is engaged.

After a short while it starts to hunt for food such as insects and moths while on the wing with its large open mouth, hence its other name "goat-sucker". Years ago some people thought they suckled milk from grazing goats.

Another noise the Nightjar makes is a cracking sound as it claps its wings beneath the body.

Its hawk-like appearance while flying and its grey brown plumage plus whiskers around the beak, makes them, as I mentioned, strange looking birds.

The male has white wing tips and if you ever get to watch Nightjars, try holding a white handkerchief above your head and if lucky you may attract a bird to fly overhead and around you. This will give you a better chance to get a closer look at this strange but fascinating bird.

Above: Side on!

Below: Side by side (chicks)!

So next year when they return from Africa it's well worth a visit to Horsell or Chobham Common to watch the interesting antics of the Nightjar. But if you do, be sure to look where you are treading for what may look like a piece of wooden bark could just be the bird you're looking for!

Farm Alarm!

Most of our larger farms are said by certain wildlife organisations, to be one of the major reasons for the decline of certain birds.

Because I covered one of the smaller farms in my previous book *"Seeing Is Believing"*, I thought it might be too much of a repeat to write about it in detail again. But I must stress without such farms even more habitat and birdlife would be lost, especially ground nesting birds. So I've decided to dedicate eight pages of bird photographs that I've taken on one such small farm in Laleham.

Left: A Yellow Wagtail from West Africa.

Above: Lapwings still flourish on the farm.

Below: There is a healthy number of Ringed Plovers.

Above & left: Little Ringed Plovers still make a show every year.

Above: The Corn Bunting used to return annually.

Left: Crowned Cranes paid the farm a winter visit

Below: Even Clouded Yellows make an appearance some years.

Above: A Meadow Pipits' hideaway!

Left: The Skylarks very often have a late brood.

Above right: The odd Whinchat passes through.

Lower right: Garden Warblers sometimes show up.

"Some of the farms hedgerows inhabitants".

Main picture: The hide I take most of my photographs from.

Upper left: Linnet.

Lower left: Greenfinch.

Below: Dunnock.

Upper & lower right: A pair of Chaffinches.

Remembering The River Ash

OCTOBER

FOLLOWING on from Farm Alarm! what little streams and rivers we have left, should be maintained and cared for. One such river, the Ash, is an example of terrible neglect. When I moved to Shepperton, it ran clear and true. Every so often two men, who I think were employed by the river authority, would wade the length of the river, cutting back reeds and generally keeping it clean. It was a river with an abundance of wildlife ranging from the little Water Vole to the much larger Otter. Waterfowl such as Mallards, Coots, Moorhens, Dabchicks and the graceful Swan nested amongst its bankside vegetation. Grey Wagtails, Reed Warblers, Sedge Warblers, Reed Buntings, Whitethroats etc., also made it their home in the breeding season. I used to watch the eels and elvers running upstream, a time when the Herons would appear in numbers to take their share. When the Mayflies hatched you could watch the Dace, Chub and even the odd Trout rise for them on a warm evening. This was also the time when I would try to tempt a fish with rod, line, and an artificial fly. Swallows flew along its length capturing insects and if you were lucky the Kingfisher would show itself like a turquoise flash as it sped by.

Those were good days, but now, no longer do the two men cut back the reeds so the river is sometimes reduced to a trickle. I still take the occasional walk along its banks but it makes me as choked and distressed as the river itself.

This has led me to write a poem of protest which I hope, one day, might just help to rescue the River Ash.

Left: The Heron loved Elvers.

Above right: Swans still nest on the River Ash.

The River (TR)Ash

The water looks skywards, gasping for air
  as dense choking reeds cause it despair.
Piles of rubbish form to make it a mess
  causing this river continual stress.
It's an everlasting effort to pass
  all the bottles of plastic and glass
Where once laid a resident pike
  now lays an old rusty bike.
With all this litter there seems no place
  for Chub, Roach, Perch and the silvery
  Dace.
A Heron stands with just one wish
  that below this garbage may swim a fish.
This spring the Moorhen, Coot and Duck
  must try to nest among this muck.

The pair of Swans that nest each year
will soon give up and disappear.
The beautiful Kingfisher that flies this
  stream
  will surely become a distant dream.
The powers that be must take heed
  of the river that once flowed with speed.
They must clean it up at any cost
  before another piece of Shepperton is lost.
We must think of our children who may
  never see
  this little river running clean and free.
All they will know is this river of trash
  that once flowed through Shepperton and
  once called…The Ash.

Derek Belsey

A family of Mallards feed as the river is reduced to a trickle.

Reed Warblers have almost disappeared

Cor, Luv a Duck !

NOVEMBER

BECAUSE of the wet weather this month not too much has been happening on the bird scene, unless you're a duck, which reminds me of a short story from a few years ago that I would like to share with you.

The River Thames, in the close vicinity of The Red Lion and Ship Hotel, holds many wildlife memories for me. Like the morning when walking back home from the newsagents with our dog, Freda.

On approaching one of the small cottages between The Red Lion and The Ship I was met by a seemingly distraught woman, who told me of a female mallard that had pecked on her back door. On opening it the duck had proceeded to walk through her cottage, followed closely by her new family of 10 ducklings.

Once the duck had got them into the front garden she then had to contemplate crossing Russell Road – and at 8am that's no mean feat. I said to the woman, who now seemed a little calmer, that if I could catch the duck and she could put the ducklings into a container, between us we could get them safely across the road and release them into the river.

All she could find was a washing basket. "It will have to do," I said and, after telling Freda to stand guard, I tried to corner the duck. As it happened it did not take long and with her firmly under my arm I told the woman to pick up the ducklings while I held up the traffic so she could get across the road.

Right: Freda stood guard.

The ducklings await their trip in a washing basket.

I stood in the middle of the road with the duck under my arm trying to explain our predicament to an enormous gravel lorry driver.

Cars behind him started to pump their horns but above all the noise I could hear the woman shouting: "I can't pick them up, they keep wriggling". I apologised to the driver, (his reply was unprintable) and returned to the front garden to once again pacify the woman.

Then, with the duck still under my arm, I picked up the ducklings one by one and placed them into the washing basket. Once more I approached the side of the road with one quacking duck under one arm and under the other the washing basket containing 10 "Jack-in-the-box" ducklings.

The first vehicle to stop was (yes you've guessed it) another gravel lorry. I sheepishly nodded my thanks and crossed the road to the river's edge. I released the duck, who called to her family, and one by one they waddled out of the washing basket to her side before dropping some five feet into the river below.

She then swam off happily with her family close behind her. Mission accomplished I turned to look back across the road to see my patient dog where I had left her, but the woman was nowhere to be seen. I could only think that she had returned to the comfort of her cottage to gather her nerves together.

I continued home with Freda, chuckling to myself and wondering what the gravel lorry drivers had said to their mates over breakfast about the idiot they had encountered with the washing basket, hanging his ducks out to dry!

The Author

38

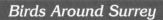

Winter Wagtail is a Real Wag

DECEMBER

YOU may read in many bird surveys that, because of modern farming methods, one of the Pied Wagtails' main sources of food has been depleted.

Obviously Bransden's Farms at Laleham and Lyne do not come into this category because at this time of the year I watch flocks of more than 100 Pied Wagtails, along with other birds, feeding on the fields.

I think the RSPB should make such farms an example to others and maybe they might just follow suit.

Now I've got that off my chest, I will get back to our little black and white bird with its ever-wagging tail.

Normally you will see Wagtails in pairs but, as I've just pointed out, this time of year they become very communal and in early evening will fly to the same roost, sometimes in their hundreds.

One such place locally was in the grounds of Birds Eye at Walton.

Some years ago I found several hundred roosting in some bullrushes in the gravel pit at the rear of my house.

In the breeding season they again pair up and become more secretive, nesting in the most peculiar places. I've found them in old car engines, cranes, piles of scrap metal, cavities in walls and even an old disused bread bin.

An over eager family of Pied Wagtails.

A real mouthful.

A most adventurous pair built their nest beneath the seat of a tractor on Bransden's Farm. When the young hatched, both parent birds took turns in flying up and under the seat to feed them while the tractor driver ploughed the fields.

I find the Pied Wagtail one of the most interesting birds because of the antics it gets up to. Most amusing is to watch a cock bird displaying to his own reflection in anything from a shop window to car wing mirrors. His courtship displays are just as amusing as he chases a female before posturing in front of her with head and wings lowered and tail spread out.

On a good year Wagtails can have up to three broods, with a high success rate. I think this is because of their unusual nest sites, which make them hard to locate by the cunning Magpies.

So over the early part of the New Year, whilst walking off the excesses of the festive season you're sure to see our resident Robins, but keep a look out for the Pied Wagtail and please continue to feed the garden birds.

Help Them to Box Clever

JANUARY

NOW is the time of year when more birds visit our gardens for food. But if you take a closer look, you'll see that certain birds are pairing up, with the males becoming more dominant as they chase a prospective mate.

I've received many phone calls lately about Blue Tits and Great Tits flying in and out of people's bird boxes.

Well, now is also the time of year when the tits start looking for suitable nesting sites so, I hope you have cleaned out your nest boxes.

This is most important for although most birds will build their nest on top of last year's, the wet and cold Spring we had in 2000 meant many young birds died in the nest.

This may have caused disease, so be on the safe side and give your box a good spring clean.

Another question I'm often asked is: "Where should I site a nest box in the garden?" I've found that over the years individual birds decide what nest box to use.

I have three in my garden and most years at least two are used, one of

Right: A winter Blue Tit.

41

them being in direct sunlight for most of the day.

This contrasts with other people I know, who have nest boxes in the so-called correct position and never get a pair of nesting birds to use them.

Throughout the winter months most tits are sociable and will give you hours of pleasure with their amusing feeding antics around the bird table and peanuts.

But it's not long before other thoughts enter their minds and the chase begins! When a pair have sorted out their differences and claim their right to one of our nest boxes, up to 14 eggs are laid.

After two weeks of incubation most of the eggs produce young, which coincides with the emergence of caterpillars in the oak trees and hawthorn bushes.

The following three weeks both parent birds are kept busy feeding up to 8,000 of these caterpillars and insects to their ever-hungry family.

Unfortunately, when the young tits leave the safety of the nest box, many are taken by Jays and the increasing population of Magpies. I've witnessed this for many years and it's getting worse even though some people and bird organisations will disagree with me.

The young tits that survive this murderous onslaught will, in the

autumn, join up with other tits and finches to form parties that flit from tree to tree. Then next year it's their turn to find a mate and lay claim to one of our nest boxes.

Left: Swinging time for a Blue Tit.

Right: A winter Great Tit.

Shopping Around for Waxwings

FEBRUARY

ONCE again this month my phone has been a hotline on our local birdlife. The calls were very varied, including details of Blue Tits displaying to their own reflection in callers' windows, a squirrel that had practically destroyed a nesting box, and a sighting by Mick Streeter of more than 300 Linnets in a field in Ashford.

I met Mick, who showed me the birds, which was very pleasing as Linnets have been on the decline locally in recent years.

But the two most interesting calls came from Sandra James and Dave Pope, who told me about a small flock of Waxwings that had been in Tesco's car park at Brooklands for about three weeks.

I decided to read up a few facts about Waxwings before paying a visit to Tesco. It seems that sometimes, every few years, several thousand of these birds visit Britain from their far-off breeding grounds in Northern Europe.

It's also been recorded that in 1957 seven Waxwings stripped the berries on 100 sq. ft. of cotoneaster on a cottage, with one bird eating roughly its own weight in berries in just two and a half hours!

Armed with binoculars and camera, I drove to Brooklands, only to find all the rowan trees had been stripped bare. It was 7.30am, the sky was overcast, with not a Waxwing in sight.

I sat in my car wondering whether I should have stayed in bed, when 24 Waxwings appeared from nowhere to drink from a puddle no further than 12 ft. away from me, revealing what beautiful birds they are.

They have red, white and yellow markings on their wings, a bright yellow end of tail, black throat, pinkish brown underneath, chestnut and grey above, with a distinctive crest on their heads.

The sun came out – and so did a lot more binocular and camera-clutching birdwatchers! I took another look around and I could make out four

Left: The Waxwings settled in my tree.

trees at the other end of the car park which still had a few berries left.

I decided to walk over to them with my camera, but with little confidence in getting a photograph.

The Waxwings soon returned, but not to the tree I had chosen. They circled above one of the others, before dropping into it for no more than 30 seconds of frantic feeding. Then they flew off, only to return to my tree ten minutes later. This time I was ready for them.

As I emptied my camera of film the birds emptied yet another rowan tree of berries. It was now time to bid the other bird-watchers farewell and to leave for home.

As I did I could not help thinking to myself that future shopping trips to Tesco would never be the same. No Waxwings, no binoculars and no clicking cameras, just cars and the occasional clicking of the old unstable shopping trolley. But I will have a wonderful memory of some wonderful Waxwings, thanks to the 'phone calls from Sandra James and Dave Pope.

A real bonus picture.

It's Cooing Doesn't Grate Me

MARCH

WHILE relaxing in our lounge the other morning a familiar sound came from the fireplace, which prompted me to write about this month's bird, the Collared Dove.

Each year, I have a pair that nest in one of the conifers but, before they do so, the cock bird woos his mate from the top of the chimney stack. Thus the familiar sound from the fireplace.

Most people accept these doves as being native to Britain, but in fact the first one was not recorded in England until 1952. About 50 years ago, the nearest Collared Dove to our shores was in Yugoslavia, whereas they now are in every corner of Great Britain.

Though they are quite common now, I still love to see them in my garden. I've noticed in recent years that sparrowhawks have become quite partial to them and I find the remains of many a kill throughout the spring and summer months.

The cock bird woos his mate from my chimney.

Above: I love to see the Collared Dove in my garden.

Once a pair of doves have mated, they build a flat nest of twigs, usually well up in a tree or large bush. Two eggs are laid as early as March, through to September. Unfortunately, many are taken by predators, so it's not uncommon some years for up to five broods to be attempted.

Incubation is about 14 days, which is shared by both birds. When hatched, the young are fed for another 18 days before leaving the security of their nest. I use the word "security" but it's during this period that they become vulnerable to the ever-present Magpies.

I'm sorry to mention the Magpie yet again, but I only write about what I see, which can be very distressing at times. Many eggs and young are taken and, when the adult birds try to defend them, they are then attacked by the Magpies.

One such pair had their eyes pecked out and I had to kill them to put the birds out of their misery – not the first time I have been forced to take such terrible action.

Those that do survive usually find their way to our garden tables to feed alongside other garden birds. Their main food supply is grain and the seeds of wild weeds.

I've also watched them with the larger Ringed Doves (Wood Pigeons), stripping many an elderberry bush or tree.

Hopefully, my pair of Collared Doves will be successful this spring in the conifers and bring their family to my garden bird table.

Such a Charming Bird

APRIL

BECAUSE of the terrible outbreak of foot-and-mouth, I appreciated even more the chance of a walk around one of our local farms recently.

Even more rewarding was the sighting of more than 80 Meadow Pipits, an equal number of Linnets and the first Yellow Wagtail to arrive from West Africa. While Lapwings, Ringed Plovers and Skylarks were all performing their courtship displays.

But the most pleasing sight for me was 15 Goldfinches sitting in a small alder tree.

When I first moved to Shepperton it was not an uncommon sight to see flocks of between 250-300 Goldfinches, Greenfinches and Linnets feeding together on thistle heads during the autumn and winter months. Now most of the habitat has disappeared and so have the large flocks of Finches.

This month's bird has got to be the colourful Goldfinch.

At the end of the last century, Goldfinches were being trapped by the thousands for the cage bird trade. I have read that in 1860 about 132,000 of these beautiful birds were being caught a year near Worthing in Sussex.

It was also reported that a young lad took 480 in a single morning. But now trapping is illegal, the Goldfinch survived extinction and although, as I mentioned I no longer see them in their hundreds, it was especially nice to see those 15 birds the other day.

I shall, as I normally do in early May, be looking out for the odd pair displaying in courtship. This usually takes place near their nest site with the male drooping, partially opening his wings and swaying side-to-side, showing his bright yellow wing flashes.

The female then does all the nest building, with small roots, moss, lichen and a lining of wool and hair. The male escorts her all the time during this period.

Five to six eggs are then laid, which are incubated by both parents for 12-13 days. For the following 14 days the young are fed on a mixture of seeds from thistle, burdock, dandelion and other weeds, along with the odd insect or two.

Usually two broods are attempted and on a good year sometimes a third.

Left: The Goldfinch show its true colours.

Above right: The first Yellow Wagtail arrives.

At the end of summer the Goldfinches gather into small flocks which are known as "charms", which leads me on to a small poem I wrote a few years ago.

> Sunlight catches the yellow and red
> On the Goldfinches body and head.
> They're seen in pairs when raising a brood
> But when that's over they alter their mood.
> They gather in flocks on many a farm
> When Goldfinches are then known as a charm.
>
> *Derek Belsey*

A Muddy Marvel

MAY

I RECENTLY visited Cliff Reddick, a friend and fellow birdwatcher who has 20 nest boxes in his garden, of which 16 are being used. The inhabitants include Blue Tits, Great Tits, Marsh Tits, Starlings and this month's bird – the Nuthatch.

The Nuthatch favours woodland habitat and if you are lucky enough to live close to one of these areas you may look on this bird as being quite common. But they were more widespread many years ago until they started to disappear from Central London, mainly due to atmospheric pollution.

This is a shame because the Nuthatch is a bird of many curious behaviours, such as being the only British bird that climbs down trees head first. It has a wide range of call notes that can resemble the sound of a Long-Tailed Tit to the chatter of a Kestrel. It also wedges nuts into the bark of a tree before splitting them open with accurate blows from its beak.

Left: A Nuthatch at Cliff's bird box.

Right: The Nuthatch climbs down the tree.

But its most fascinating behaviour is commonly called muddying up. This happens when a pair of birds select a nesthole and then reduce the size of it by plastering the entrance with mud. This they will also do to a man-made nest box such as Cliff has in his garden.

This reminded me of a few years ago whilst I was playing a round of golf. I caught a glimpse of a Nuthatch as it flew past and noticed it was carrying something black in its beak. I took a short break from the golf to take a closer look. It did not take me long to find its nesthole

about eight feet up in a nearby tree. But the hole had a black surround to it, which turned out to be Tarmac.

The bird had found a pile of it which was being used for a path on the golf course and was possibly finding it easier than collecting mud.

It would also give the nest hole protection from predators such as the Great Spotted Woodpecker, who will sometimes take the young of Nuthatches.

Distinguishing features of the Nuthatch are the black eye stripe, white throat, bluish grey upper parts and buff underparts.

They nest in natural holes in trees or garden nest boxes which they line with flakes of bark or dead leaves.

In late April to May, six to 10 eggs are laid, which the female incubates for about 14 days. The nestlings are fed by both parents and fly after approximately 24 days.

Their diet consists mainly of hazel nuts, acorns, beetles, caterpillars and small insects.

So long as there are trees we should be able to watch the Nuthatch climbing down them to feed on the peanut holders in our gardens.

P.S. Phone calls this month were plenty, reporting such birds as Whitethroats, Grasshopper Warblers and Nightingales etc. Larger species included a pair of Buzzards flying over Shepperton, Greylag Geese and a pair of Egyptian Geese that chose to nest in an old owl box 20 feet up in a tree at Lyne.

51

Planning Gives
IT the PIP

JUNE

IT saddens me to write about yet another bird that will soon disappear from our area, the Meadow Pipit.

The front page of the Sunbury and Shepperton edition of the Herald on July 5 told of the proposed new village health centre – and I already know that neighbouring land is up for sale. Other vital areas at risk include the area around Chertsey Marina.

How much more of our wildlife is going to dwindle away to extinction?

Thirty years ago the Pipit, along with Linnets, Goldfinches, Greenfinches, Little Ringed Plovers, Redshanks, Partridges, Yellow

Wagtails, Kingfishers, Skylarks and the like, and possibly one of the largest Sand Martin colonies in the country, could be seen in Shepperton.

Alas, the by-pass put paid to most of these birds and now, if the planners get their way, I will have to refer to a bird book to explain to my grandchildren what a Meadow Pipit looked like.

All our meadows and grasslands are being taken, so we need more people like Jill Stevens and her Civic Pride group, who restore and introduce new habitat for our local wildlife.

They help the regional officer for the British Trust for Ornithology, Hugh Evans, who records the numbers of birds in our area.

I cannot overstress how much these two organisations need our support, for they are probably nature's last hope in our surrounding areas.

With those very important points over, it was very nice to see a pair of Meadow Pipits nesting in an area next to the by-pass, which they have been using for several years.

I spent even more time watching them this year, as it could be their last in this vicinity.

As usual the cock bird was very wary and used several ploys to lead me away from its nesting site. One was to perch up on a prominent point with a beak full of feed and move from bush to bush until he was some 100 metres from where I first spotted him.

Then after about another five minutes, he swallowed the feed and flew off out of sight. I've got to know this ploy and I found the nest which contained five healthy chicks.

I cannot divulge my methods of detecting the nest (albeit legitimately) for organisations such as the RSPB frown upon it. But it helps me to record their success rate, even if it is small.

The Meadow Pipit is a prime target for visiting Cuckoos, so it's just as well their numbers are also down this year.

To recognise the Meadow Pipit, look out for its upper parts of olive brown and dark brown marking with its breast of speckled white feathers. The nest is always well-hidden in vegetation or grass and three to five eggs are laid, which the female incubates. The nestlings leave the nest after 14 days, being fed by both

parents on a diet of insects, beetles, craneflies, caterpillars, grasshoppers and spiders etc. Next spring I shall return along with the Meadow Pipits, subject to planning permission.

P.S. For further information about Spelthorne Civic Pride call Jill Stevens daytime 01932 829460 or 01932 564543.
BTO call Hugh Evans 01932 227781.

Left: Meadow Pipit resting a leg.

Above right: Meadow Pipit on both legs.

Spot the Flycatcher

JULY

A FTER writing last month about the dismal future for Meadow Pipits in these parts, it is a pleasant change to write about a bird that has shown up again after an absence of six to eight years, the Spotted Flycatcher.

In fact, there has been a 78% decline nationally over the past 30 years.

Several people have phoned to tell me of sightings and I have found three pairs nesting successfully. One of these was spotted by Hugh Evans of the BTO, not more than 600 yards from where I live. It was an opportunity not to be missed so, armed with camera and tripod, I paid this pair of Flycatchers a visit.

After watching them for a while it seemed their favourite perch before flying up to the nest was either a hanging flower basket or the aerial of a car. It was a fascinating hour or so watching and filming them catching insects in mid-air. They would take anything from small flies and wasps to quite large dragonflies.

To me, this was one of the highlights of this year's breeding season because, as I've mentioned, they had disappeared from these parts for the last six to eight years.

I hope this is going to be a good omen for the future. If it is and you would like to see these little birds performing their aerobatics while chasing flying insects, here are a few pointers that may help.

They usually arrive in this country in late May and stay until September. They are not actually spotted but grey with white underparts and dark grey streaks on their head and breast. Being quiet little birds they are easily missed, but once you have detected a pair, many hours of brilliant bird-watching may be had.

Both birds will pick out a vantage point to watch for flying insects and if you can get close enough, you can hear their beaks click together when they capture one.

Left: Aerial Flycatcher.

Right: Floral Flycatcher.

Above: The Flycatcher takes a break.

An untidy nest is built with wool, moss and hair which is held together with cobwebs, each bird helping in the construction.

They usually choose a ledge or creeper for this purpose but I have found them in wall cavities, holes in trees and even an old tin can.

Another nest reported to me this year was on top of an electric junction box in a garage.

Four to five eggs are then laid. They are green or blue with reddish-brown freckles. The female does most of the incubation for about 13 days. Once hatched, the young are fed by both parents and fly after 12 to 13 days. This is the time they become spotted looking, but this disappears when they get their full adult plumage.

In a good summer, they sometimes raise two broods. Next year, I hope even more people call me about sightings of these beautiful little birds and that should help to reassure me that the Spotted Flycatchers are back in force.

P.S. I've had numerous phone calls this month, including one from David Pope who saw more than 500 Canada Geese, along with one Snow Goose and a White-Fronted, grazing in a field at Thorpe.

Many others reported the welcome return of House Sparrows, with Stan Talbot counting more than 150 in his garden. He also told me of three Wood Sandpipers that had been spotted in the area.

Clive Poole, a local ornithologist and BTO member, reported a juvenile Hobby on August 15 hunting over the Meadow Pipits' territory and along the Black Ditch for dragonflies.

On the downside, a lot more mink have shown themselves.

A Long Distance Haul for Swallows

AUGUST

ONCE again, it is a pleasure to write that the Swallow has also had a good year, probably due to favourable weather conditions.

So has its smaller cousin, the House Martin, but alas Sand Martins seem to be fewer locally. This is mostly due to the lack of suitable nesting sites.

There is a saying that "one swallow does not make a summer" as they arrive here from Africa in ones and twos at the end of March or early April.

It's not until mid April that they appear in greater numbers – and summer is then on the way.

The Swallow is a bird I have studied for a number of years and I'm sorry to say it is yet another which is in decline. There are many reasons given for this but I feel it's because of the modern world we live in, e.g. larger farms, spraying methods and fewer flying insects.

There are now fewer smaller farms, stables and old outhouse buildings for them to nest in. Those that do pay us a visit fly all the way from South Africa with some travelling further north, even as far as the Shetland Isles.

Below: The Swallow takes a rest.

Left: Such a lovely picture.

Above: House Martins collecting mud for nest building.

Having done the trip to the Shetlands from Shepperton by car and ferry I can appreciate the endurance flight these small birds undertake each year.

Some people mistake Swallows for House Martins, but if you take a closer look there is a distinct difference. House Martins are a blue/black colour above and have a white underneath and rump, while the Swallow is more streamlined with a forked tail. Its upper parts are of a similar blue with a chestnut forehead and breast.

As I've stated, though they start arriving as early as March they do not start nesting until May through to August. Both birds help to build a bowl-shaped nest of mud and grass, which is then lined with feathers.

The usual site for this, is on a rafter or ledge in a building. I've found many a nest built on a fixed light, which does not seem to disturb the sitting bird when switched on or off.

Three to six eggs, white and heavily marked with red/brown blotches, are laid, with the hen bird incubating for about 15 days.

The nestlings are fed by both parents on a diet of small flying insects but sometimes, larger dragonflies and butterflies.

The young leave the nest after 18-20 days. This is a good time to watch as their parents teach them to hunt between feeding forays.

You may also see the whole family perched up on a telephone wire preening themselves before taking off like a squadron of jet fighter planes.

I've spent many an evening watching their aerial displays, especially over one of our many gravel pits, sometimes picking insects off the water's surface. I hope to watch them as they 'make a summer' for many more years.

P.S. There were some very interesting sightings this month including Egrets on Staines Moor, an Osprey carrying a fish in its talons over Shepperton and Hobbies hunting over Chertsey Meads.

Kestrels' Kingdom

SEPTEMBER

Only a few weeks ago I was very fortunate to watch a pair of Kestrels hunting over some open land, which brings me nicely onto one of the most-often-asked questions "What is the difference between a Sparrowhawk and a Kestrel"?

The only similarity is they are both birds of prey and that's where it ends. They both hunt is different ways, with the Sparrowhawk usually flying low and fast, before lunging at a startled bird, which can be as small as a Blue Tit or as large as a Wood Pigeon.

Whereas the Kestrel will watch from a vantage point before hovering, then dropping onto an unsuspecting mouse, young rat, vole, frog, earthworm, large insect or sometimes a small bird.

There was a pair I watched earlier this year on a local farm, taking Lapwing chicks. This was unfortunate as Lapwings are birds very much on the decline.

The Kestrel, like the Sparrowhawk, is protected by law but, unlike other birds of prey, it is not persecuted as much. The farmers realise they help keep down the population of small rodents and harmful insects. Most gamekeepers feel the same so they don't mind the occasional chick being taken.

In recent years the Kestrel has also become an urban bird and many now nest in the heart of London, with the House Sparrow being their main food supply.

Left: A Kestrel at its nest.

Above: One of the lucky Kestrels that Jim saved.

Many years ago while travelling on a London bus at Marble Arch, I saw a Kestrel plunge down onto a busy pavement to take a sparrow.

Sparrowhawks usually build a new nest each year but Kestrels will use the same nesting site year after year. These can range from a high building, a cliff ledge, a tree hole or an old nest of another bird. I once found a pair nesting in a window box in a holiday apartment and by looking from the flat roof top, I could see five well-grown chicks.

I obviously spent many hours watching the chicks being fed as I don't often get that sort of opportunity.

A few years ago a local tree surgeon felled an old tree, unaware Kestrels were nesting in it. Jim, a friend of mine, saved the young and with little knowledge, hand-reared them before successfully releasing the birds into the wild. That's another story, but I managed to take some photographs for the record book.

If in the future you would like to see a Kestrel and don't know of any nesting sites, take a short trip along the motorway and as soon as you spot a bird hovering over it, you've seen a Kestrel!

Birds of Prey Have Their Day

I HAD planned to write about the hard time our smaller birds have had this year, what with the wet springtime weather and the increase of birds of prey.

Then a phone call from Mike Ballard (a fellow birdwatcher) about a family of Hobbies he had been watching on Chertsey Meads, prompted me to carry on from last month's article on birds of prey in the area.

Starting with the Hobby, which is a small falcon that nests in June. The hatching of its young coincides with the peak time for Swallows and House Martins. This means an abundance of food. Along with their other favourites, dragonflies, which they pluck from the air and eat whilst still flying, makes watching them very rewarding.

Thanks for the phone call Mike! I certainly enjoyed watching your Hobbies performing their aerobatics over the Meads.

Last year a pair of Goshawks were occasionally seen in the Shepperton and Laleham area. I was lucky enough to verify the sightings as I watched one being mobbed by Lapwings I was photographing at the time.

Kestrels seem to be holding their own and it's not an uncommon sight to see one hovering overhead as it searches for a small mouse or vole.

As I wrote last month, Sparrowhawks are definitely on the increase.

Moving on to larger birds, Buzzards have now moved into Surrey and I know of two breeding pairs not too far away, which probably means there are others. They feed

Left: Buzzards are getting closer!

Above right: Colourful but cunning – Jays.

mainly on carrion but will take live birds and small animals, especially when feeding their young.

Add to this list the Red Kites that have been released in bordering counties of Buckinghamshire and Berkshire, and we have an upsurge in birds of prey.

Let's not forget the odd Tawny Owl and Little Owl that are unfortunately on the decline locally, but still show up from time to time.

Although not classified as birds of prey, Magpies, Jays, Crows and even Great Spotted Woodpeckers take the young of other birds.

As I wrote at the start, our smaller birds do have a hard time, but I guess it's nature's way of balancing things out.

P.S. The Kingfishers on the Abbey River fledged and hopefully will return nest year to show us their magnificent turquoise blue colours as they fly low across the water.

A Trip Across The Moor

OCTOBER

I RECEIVED a phone call from Stan Talbot telling me about a pair of Egrets that had been seen on land adjacent to Staines Moor. Usually, at this time of the year, I like to take in a game of local football on a Saturday. But it was such a nice day I decided to follow up Stans' call and give the Moor a visit. I was glad I did, because on arriving I was pleasantly surprised to find it empty of people and huge beds of irises had re-established themselves.

This was how I remembered the moor some 40 years ago when I lived back in London.

Full of renewed enthusiasm I set off from the Staines end of the moor and within two minutes I spotted my first bird, a female Stonechat.

I sat and watched her feeding for a while, before seeing a Reed Bunting being scolded by the cock Stonechat. This was a good start as Stonechats have virtually disappeared from this area.

After a short break, I carried on across the

Left: I heard and saw the Green Woodpecker.

Above: A female Reed Bunting was the second bird I saw.

moor, taking note of such birds as Swans, Moorhens and Mallards along the stretch of the River Colne.

As well as Green Woodpeckers, Mistle Thrushes, Blackbirds, Wood Pigeons, Robins, Linnets, Greenfinches and a beautiful "charm" of Goldfinches to name but a few.

Now in the middle of the moor, I watched a pair of Kestrels hunting, as higher in the sky a huge flock of Swallows and House Martins were feeding on the wing before flying back to South Africa.

I had almost reached the Stanwell end of the moor when a pair of Redshanks took to the air in alarm, which put up a flock of Meadow Pipits.

Sitting down for a rest, I realised I should have paid more visits to this wildlife haven, when I saw flocks of Blue Tits, Great Tits and Long Tailed Tits flitting throughout the waterside trees and vegetation.

These were followed by three Blackcaps and it was while I was watching these, that I caught sight of two white patches through the trees; the Egrets that Stan had phoned me about.

I had time for a closer look through my binoculars before they flew out of sight. I thought that was my "mission accomplished" but then, in the shallow water, I made out some other birds and once more through the binoculars, I watched Gadwall, Teal, Common Sandpipers and at least 16 Snipe, that were so at ease, some were even taking a nap in the warmth of the autumn sun.

There was also a wader that I could not identify, but then waders have never been my strongest point!

On leaving the moor I met the first person I had seen in the best part of three hours. A veritable wildlife sanctuary in the midst of the fast hustle of every day life.

The Redshank gave an alarm call!

The first bird I spotted was a female Stonechat.

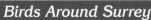

Tough Time for a Tufted Duck

NOVEMBER

BEFORE the 19th century Tufted Ducks did not breed in Britain but now they are our most common diving duck and nest almost everywhere.

At this time of year our resident birds are joined by thousands from Iceland and Northern Europe to form huge parties on reservoirs, lakes, gravel pits and other large expanses of water.

This is also the time when they mix freely with other waterfowl such as Coots, Mallards and Pochards.

Tufted Ducks are usually timid birds but once established on park lakes become much bolder. I've had them take bread from my hand in such places as Bushy Park and Hampton Court. In their natural wild environment they become even more secretive, especially in the breeding season. You can recognise the male by his black and white plumage and long drooping crest.

The female is brown with a much smaller crest. Their courtship display is simple but amusing with the male tilting his head back while making a sort of whistling sound. His mate replies with a growling call then dips her beak repeatedly into the water.

A nest is then built close to the water's edge and lined with down before up to 14 eggs are laid in late May to June.

The female incubates them for about 24 days and when hatched the ducklings can swim and dive after a few hours. She then teaches them the skills of catching insects, frogs spawn, mussels, small fish and water plants before they fly after just six weeks.

There is a pair of Tufted Ducks locally that I watch every year and I feel they've got to know me. I've found their nest twice and on both occasions she has sat tight on her eggs when I've been only a few feet away.

Earlier this year I was watching them and not too far away a pair of Little Grebes displaying. I could hardly believe my eyes when the male Tufted Duck escorted his mate to the water's edge before swimming off.

After a few minutes I saw her approaching me through the undergrowth. I sat motionless as she settled down on 10 eggs just two yards from me. I slowly moved away to leave her in peace and carry out her parental duties. I checked on the nest over the following days hoping she would not be disturbed or discovered by a fox. Then one day she was gone and all that remained were a few broken egg shells. I feared the worst for there was no sign of either adult bird.

Feeling a bit down, I sat and watched the Little Grebe approach its nest and, after

Left: Tufted Ducks mix with Pochards.

uncovering the eggs, hop on to it to settle down. That was when a particular Tufted Duck swam past to show me her family of nine newly-born ducklings. This was one of those wonderful moments in bird watching when I believed I had been accepted into their world. I hope so because I shall return next year to watch over them again.

Meanwhile this month, on the same stretch of water a rare visitor dropped in to shelter from a bout of rough weather. The Grey Phalarope, a small wading bird and a regular passage migrant from Iceland, was spotted by Jonathan Lambert, who phones me regularly about sightings.

This is his best yet and I managed to get a few photographs for him before the bird left to continue its journey to the South Atlantic to join other Phalaropes and winter there. Jonathan also told me of a Short-eared Owl he had seen recently.

Above: Jonathan's best sighting – a Grey Phalarope.

Below: An unforgettable swimpast.

The Little Grebe hops onto its nest.

The male used to escort his mate to the nest.

Sunday Morning in Bushy Park

I TRY to get at least one visit to Bushy Park each year, usually in the rutting season. At that time there is always some action amongst the deer, even though I have to tread cautiously because you are warned not to venture too close during the rutt. Many people use the park to pursue their hobbies – anglers, horse riders, joggers, artists, ramblers, model boat enthusiasts, picnickers, horticulturists etc., and of course, birdwatchers. But if you can get to one of the more quieter spots in the park and let nature come to you, it's amazing what you might see. For there is an abundance of birdlife, ranging from tiny Goldcrests to the larger Herons.

This year autumn has seemed a long time coming and it was not until the back end of November that I paid the park a visit. The day I chose turned out to be the right one as the following events will prove.

On arrival at 8 a.m. on Sunday morning, there was still a heavy frost laying and a slight mist, so I decided to look for the deer. Whilst doing so I passed some visiting Redwings feeding on berries and a pair of Stonechats flitting about in the bracken. I soon found some deer which were very photogenic. I even got a photograph of a Magpie foraging on the back of a large Stag. Then I was off to try and find a Heron and again good fortune looked down on me for in the distance I could see one by the side of a stream. Approaching the Heron with much caution I managed some

Right: Model boat enthusiasts enjoying *their* hobby.

reasonable photographs until I got within 20 feet of the bird. The Heron had obviously seen a fish and was preoccupied but I could see he had one eye on me. After capturing the picture I wanted, I retreated slowly to allow the Heron to capture the fish <u>he</u> wanted.

By this time the park was filling up and the sun had burnt off the mist. With film still left in my camera I decided to use it up on some of the parks' waterfowl. I found some Gadwall, Widgeon and Pintail ducks that were very co-operative and it was not long before I reached the end of the film. Quickly reloading my camera I carried on taking pictures until a dog leapt into the water to retrieve a lump of wood that its owner had thrown in. A less than polite conversation followed with the dog owner saying "the park is for everyone", I replied "can you swim?" – I never did get his reply as he hurriedly left one irate birdwatching photographer and a pond devoid of ducks. Because the light was now so good I would have felt cheated if I left the park, so a visit to another resident, a Tawny Owl was in order.

Above: Photogenic Deer.

Right: A Magpie gets all *beHIND!*

This turned out to be a real bonus for there were two owls sitting in the nest hole. Although the owls were some 50 feet up in an old oak tree, my camera went into overdrive to capture some very rewarding photographs.

It was then that I realised how hungry I felt and it was time for breakfast but a look at my watch told me it was time for lunch. Later that afternoon with my digestive system now satisfied I decided to write this little episode hoping it might just entice you to give Bushy Park a visit.

The Heron gave a good reflection of the morning.

Glorious Gadwall.

A portrait of the Pintail.

Winter Wigeon.

The sun came out and so did the Owls.

Move Over Robins

DECEMBER

THOUGH it's the Robin that is mostly related to the festive season, each year at this time I try to mention an alternative bird. This year I've picked two – the Egyptian Goose, whose distant cousin, the "Farmyard Goose" IS related to the kitchen table, and the Ring-Necked Parakeet because I photographed one in the snow last Boxing Day!

It also gives me the chance to try and answer some of the many questions I've been asked about these species over the past years.

Firstly the Egyptian Goose. It originated from Africa but has since escaped from private wildfowl collections and has bred successfully in the wild, hence the sightings of many more that have chosen to breed locally.

Unfortunately, only a few of their goslings survive, which I think is due to the ever-present Crows who I've seen take them from unaware adults. Only two weeks ago I saw eight Egyptian Geese feeding with about 250 Canada Geese along Cowey Sale at Walton. I thought to myself at the time "If they become as successful as the Canadas, nature will be even more unbalanced."

Left: Boxing Day Parakeet.

Right: It's the Robin that's related to the Festive Season.

Above: An Egyptian Goose stands guard.

My second bird, the Ring-Necked Parakeet, is now common to gardens that have peanuts out for Blue Tits etc. As I write this article there are 10 of them on the nuts and bird table in my garden.

Again, this is a bird that has escaped from captivity and it is estimated there are now about 5,000 in our area. Many stories are told about how and where they escaped. The one I go for is that a few got out of a cage at Shepperton Studios some 30 odd years ago.

They love buds and fruit so it seems they have taken over from the orchardman's "pest," the Bullfinch. I have seen just a few Parakeets strip a large apple tree in less than a week.

They nest in tree holes, so old Woodpecker nest holes are often used and I've watched newly-excavated ones pirated, which makes the Parakeets a special enemy of the Great Spotted Woodpecker.

They are a bird that also make me contradict myself at times. For example, I have seen Sparrowhawks flying alongside flocks of Ring-Necked Parakeets, causing no alarm to them whatsoever, only to be told by someone that a Sparrowhawk quite regularly takes them from his garden as prey, leaving just a pile of feathers.

As I have already said, they usually get the better of Great Spotted Woodpeckers yet in my garden the Woodpecker rules.

I hope I've managed to answer some of the questions about my chosen festive birds, the Ring-Necked Parakeet and the Egyptian Goose. One thing I'm sure of, they will never replace the Robin on Christmas Cards, festive stamps or the occasional chocolate log.

Left: The goslings take their first swim.

A Berry Good Time for Birds

Now you see the berry.

AS I've mentioned before, Redwings are members of the thrush family and visit us each year from Northern Europe. They usually arrive here with another thrush member, the Fieldfare.

I know of some Redwings that each year make their home base at Sainsbury's Homebase in Walton. The reason? a row of bushes laden with berries that runs alongside the store's car park. I made it my aim this winter to try and capture some photographs of them.

I saw the first Redwings to arrive locally as early as October and I've been checking their winter abode ever since. It was not until just before Christmas that I saw a few on the Homebase berries. In fact, after several counts, there were only seven birds.

After watching their feeding habits while sitting in my car, it was time for my camera to go into action. I noticed that there was one dominant Redwing, who seemed less frightened of the ever-passing pedestrians and traffic.

After many patient hours I eventually got him in focus and was about to press the shutter when the viewfinder went black. Shutter jammed or locked? No! It was a lady standing in front of me asking: "What are you photographing?" I replied with a slightly-forced but hopefully convincing smile: "Your coat lady!" She apologised and carried on her way to do the Christmas shopping.

(If bird photography was always easy it would become boring).

After several visits over the Christmas period, when things were quieter, I did manage to get some very pleasing photographs while also studying the Redwings' feeding behaviour. Blackbirds also took their share of the abundance of berries as did one Fieldfare which showed itself briefly.

But in all the hours spent there I did not see one Songthrush. So it was nice to receive a phone call from a Mr Rand, of Weybridge, who told me of three that showed up in his garden this month. He even managed to find some snails, that the Thrushes enjoyed.

The Songthrush is very much on the decline and since last summer I have not seen one in my garden, which is of great concern.

Stan Talbot, of Ashford, who phones me regularly about bird sightings, has had a female Blackcap in his garden this winter.

This brings me on to another point of interest, for another friend, Dave Capon, of Shepperton has had a male Blackcap feeding on his bird table.

This goes to prove many of these little warblers now winter here. Dave also remembers Redwings being around Walton Homebase long before it was built, in fact 30 years ago.

Which again proves our visiting winter birds return each year to the same territories as do others in the springtime breeding season.

Left: Now you don't (Well just a bit maybe!).

The Blackbird takes his share of berries.

Greenfinches and Sunflower Seeds

JANUARY

TO brighten up the drab month of January

I've decided to write in short detail, about a bird that I have been watching feeding, in mixed flocks of Linnets and Meadow Pippits on my local farm recently – the Greenfinch. It's a very hardy and adaptable bird that's widespread throughout most of the British Isles. In a couple of months time I shall be waiting to hear the cock birds' familiar "Tswee" call which will whet my appetite for the following months. For this is the time of year when its plumage becomes bright green, sometimes bordering on yellow.

Many years ago as a lad, I used to find hundreds of Linnets and Greenfinches nests, but as their habitat has gradually diminished, so have the nests. Once paired up both birds build a cup-shaped nest of grass and moss which is roughly lined, usually in a bush or hedge. Four to six whitish blue and reddish brown marked eggs are then laid, which are incubated by the female for about 13 days. For the following 12–16 days both adult birds feed their young on mostly seeds and berries. This is also the time of year when whole families of Greenfinches become quite sociable, joining other birds at garden tables to feed on the never-ending supply of peanuts and bird seed. In a good year 2–3 broods may be attempted. So if like me, you want to encourage the colourful Greenfinch into your garden put out plenty of sunflower seeds – it seems to be their favourite.

Left & above: Its green is almost yellow at times.

Such a Hoot to Hear an Owl

FEBRUARY & MARCH

OVER the years the months of February and March have never been very exciting birdwise, but after looking through my notes the other day it seems it's changing. For example, Great Crested Grebes have raised chicks in February and early March.

Blue Tits and Great Tits are prospecting for suitable nesting sites much earlier. I received a phone call from a Mrs Martin of Chertsey, who told me about a pair of Robins who were building a nest in her garden on January 24th this year.

All this early activity is partly due to climatic changes which are giving us milder winters.

The frogs in my garden are already noisily pursuing their sexual activities. Another noise I've heard lately was the pleasing sound of a Tawny Owl calling to a mate.

When I first moved to Shepperton 34 years ago this was quite common until Dutch Elm disease struck and wiped out most of the Tawny Owl's habitat. Add to that the gradual disappearance of small copses, wooded parks and gardens, meaning the Owls have had to go further afield to nest.

So to hear one calling in January and being told of other sightings locally has been very encouraging.

If you go looking for Tawny Owls, a giveaway to one roosting in the daytime is noisy parties of birds such as Blackbirds and Chaffinches mobbing it. Usually the Owl will sit seemingly uninterested, until they give up and leave it in peace.

Night-time is when they become more evident as they call and hunt for food. The Owl will strike many an unsuspecting mammal with its talons. After feeding it will regurgitate a pellet made of fur and small bones.

In the past I've taken apart many of these pellets to find out the Tawny Owl's diet. It ranges from mice, young rats, voles, shrews, the occasional bird, fish and frog to smaller worms and insects.

Tawny Owls do not build nests but will take over an old tree hole or another bird's nest, especially that of a Sparrowhawk. Sometimes a squirrel's dray or an old building may be used. They have also been known to nest on the ground.

Two to four white eggs are laid in March to May, which are incubated for 28–30 days by the female. When the young hatch out they are fed mostly by the male, before being able to fly after 30–37 days.

Hearing that Tawny Owl calling the other night brought back memories of when there was a healthy population of elm trees and, equally, a good choice of small mammals on the Owl's menu. Most of these have gone and so have the Owls.

Will this be yet another bird which we will have to refer to in a picture book to explain to children in the future what it looked like? Or maybe, all the good tree planting work being carried out by Civic Pride will come to their rescue one day.

Left: A contented couple of Owls *(front cover picture)*.

Reed Bunting Revival?

APRIL

THE Reed Bunting, over the last few years, is yet another bird that has become less frequent to our area. I used to look upon them as one of the more common visitors to our shores. Some even over-wintered here and joined other resident birds at garden feeding tables. Each spring I could watch the handsome cock bird with his black head and white collar, chasing a female. Some would entice more than one female to mate, which often led to nest sharing. For the past two breeding seasons I've tried to photograph a pair of Reed Buntings for this book without any luck,

So I was pleasantly surprised at the end of this month while looking over a particular piece of scrubland, to see two cockbirds squabbling over territorial rights. But I was wrong, for close by a female was performing a distraction display to lead me away from her nest. She was shuffling along the undergrowth feigning an injured wing and her mate was seeing off a rival male.

This I've seen many times so it did not take

Right: The female did most of the feeding.

Above: The male paid the occasional visit.

very long to find the nest. As usual it was built deep down in thick vegetation, made of dry grass and lined with mostly hair. It contained five green and black marked eggs. During the incubation period of about 14 days I gradually moved a hide into the area, making sure not to get too close or disturb the Reed Buntings. This is the way fieldcraft should always be carried out, but even more so with these birds. The young will leave the nest before they are fully fledged if startled or frightened.

As I've said many times, the birds welfare and safety is always more important than any photograph. Once the eggs hatched, the nestlings were fed by both parents with a variety of insects, caterpillars, moths and beetles etc. The male made less visits to the nest as he had another mate and young not too far away. So I was doubly pleased, for not only did I get some good photography and birdwatching, but it was nice to know that two families of Reed Buntings had been reared successfully. I shall, as I always do, return to this piece of scrubland next year to watch for the return of even *more* Reed Buntings.

May Brings Very Mixed Fortunes

L IKE the weather, the bird news for May is a bit of a mixture. Most of the nesting birds I have found, such as Chaffinches, Blackbirds, Song Thrushes, Dunnocks, Wrens etc, have become the victims of Magpies.

Although our local Lapwings have reared a good number of chicks, most have been taken by resident Crows.

Canada Geese have produced more goslings than usual, which will obviously cause concern about the increase in their numbers.

Another newcomer, the Egyptian Goose looks like the bird that may start alarm bells ringing in a few years to come. I know of at least six pairs locally that have raised up to six goslings each. One pair I photographed on a late sunny afternoon this month seemed happy enough feeding and caring alongside their four goslings. Yet just two hours later they deserted their young, with the adult male attempting to kill the three-day-old goslings.

This I found so distressing I phoned the Egham Swan Sanctuary, whose team arrived at

Below: A seemingly happy family of Egyptian Geese.

the water's edge within 15 minutes to try and save them.

But by now the goslings were too frightened and all attempts to catch them failed, which left their chances of survival overnight very slim. As I have said many times before, nature can be very cruel at times.

Coots, Moorhens and Mallards seem to have fared well this spring with two reports of 19 and another of 21 ducklings. Usually most will be taken by Pike or Crows, but sometimes a family of Mallards do escape from the predators, like the pair with 11 well-grown ducklings that Barry Dix (Surrey Herald sub-

editor) and I saw while walking across Staines Moor one evening last week.

We also spotted a variety of other birds, with the added bonus of watching a Grey Plover in full summer plumage and a Dunlin feeding together by the side of a shallow pool.

A trip across the moor at any time of the year is always worth the effort, especially if followed by a couple of pints of liquid refreshment in the nearby Swan public house. With all these goings-on, once again I have left little space to cover this month's chosen bird, the Tree Creeper.

Main picture: Staines Moor

Below left: Seeing a Dunlin was a bonus.

Below right: A successful brood of ducklings.

Above: Tree Creeper busily nest building.

This little brown bird with white underparts and curved beak, is heard more than seen. It is difficult to see as it crawls up trees because its colours blend in with the colours of the bark.

In their breeding season, April to June, they build a nest behind some old loose bark on the side of a tree, which makes it hard to find. But a closer look sometimes reveals pieces of nesting material poking out of cracks in the bark. I have found the odd nest in a wall crevice and one behind some old fencing.

After a courtship display of chases, wing-shivering and courtship feeding, six eggs, white with reddish brown spots at one end, are laid.

These are incubated, mostly by the hen bird, for about 15 days. The nestlings are then fed by both adults before leaving the nest after 14 to 15 days. Some years two broods are attempted.

This year I was lucky enough to watch one pair of Tree Creepers building a nest in an old willow tree just off Felix Lane in Shepperton. It seems a Great Spotted Woodpecker was also watching and, later, raided the nest.

I have since seen the Tree Creepers carrying nesting material in a nearby area and hopefully this time they will be successful in raising a brood.

A Lot of Time for Little Owls

JUNE

THE Little Owl was introduced to this country from the continent at the end of the last century. It was not very popular with gamekeepers who thought its main diet was Pheasant and Partridge chicks. This was proved to be untrue and the Little Owl spread throughout most of England.

Being a secretive bird and standing just 8½ inches high, it's greyish brown and mottled white plumage, helps to camouflage its presence.

I knew of at least 3 pairs of Little Owls that nested locally but once again I have to report that they have all gone. It seems the further I've got into this book more species have joined the absentee list.

A pair that I was pretty confident of seeing this spring never made an appearance. So it was heartening to receive a phone call from my friend and fellow birdwatcher Cliff Reddick, about a pair that had nested in a tree hole in the Ockley area. Even better, he had worked a hide into a prominent position to watch and photograph from. Everything was going to plan with 4 white eggs being laid which were incubated by the female for about 28 days, producing 4 healthy chicks. Both parents then

continued to feed them on a diet of mostly beetles and worms with the odd small mammal thrown in. Then the weather changed and torrential rain flooded the nest hole that was just two feet off the ground. Unfortunately 2 of the young Owls died, which Cliff removed before managing to get a pile of

Right: An inquisitive look.

91

Little Owl with a little chick.

sawdust and chippings into the nest hole entrance, hoping to soak up any remaining water. Things were obviously looking grim as there were no signs of either the adults or young birds. After several visits to the site, at last! a little wet and bedraggled head appeared from the nest hole which was greeted by a reassuring call from one of the parent birds in a nearby tree. But alas, a third chick had died which made us wonder if the remaining youngster would make it.

Many sessions were shared in the hide to watch the outcome of this near total disaster. But because there was now only one surviving chick, feeding visits from the parents became less frequent, so it was not unusual to sit for up to 4 hours without seeing either adult bird. This had to be done to make sure the chick was being fed. The outcome of it was, all Cliff's work and care was rewarded, because the baby Owl fledged and after several attempts, flew up into the surrounding trees to join its much relieved parents.

Maybe next year the weather will be kinder and I will be able to return to watch the Little Owls with less concern. Whatever happens a supply of sawdust and wood-chippings will be at the ready.

Little Owl with a little beetle.

A little hero.

Memories

I hope my book has helped to make you aware of some of the birds around the Surrey area and will encourage you to go out into our countryside to discover even more.

Above left: Song Trush and young.

Above reft: Great Spotted Woodpecker.

Below: Colourful Starling.

Above: Moorhen approaches it's nest.

94

Left: Muscovy Duck and ducklings.

Above: Woodlark at the nest.

Below: Female Wheatear.

Above: Male Yellowhammer.

Below left: A family of Canada Geese

Below right: "Looks a bit fishy to me!"

ACKNOWLEDGEMENTS

My wife Patricia for her continuous understanding.

Nick Payne for his support over the years.

Charles, Clare and their staff for helping to locate nesting birds on the farm.

Jimmy (The Shrimp) for his kind donation.

Billinge Blend & Co. for their kind donation.

Mercer for his bird ringing, records and knowhow.

All the people who phoned me about bird sightings.

Everyone who bought my first 2 books and those who buy this one.

Jonathan Bingham and Peter Gallagher, two very helpful people.

Robert Antell for his patience and understanding.

David Allan for his help and belief in this publication.

Finally my good friend, Mac who did all the type-setting – my sincere thanks.

This Yellow Wagtail Brings My Book
to an End.